A TREASURY OF

MW00584084

Presented to ....

From ....

Date ....

Other books by Maulana Wahiduddin Khan

God Arises:
The Evidence of God in Nature and in Science

Woman between Islam and Western Society

God-Oriented Life

Muhammad: The Prophet of Humanity

Islam As It Is

Islam: The Voice of Human Nature

Islam: Creator of the Modern Age

Religion and Science

Indian Muslims: The Need For A Positive Outlook

Woman in Islamic Shari'ah

Tabligh Movement

Tazkirul Qur'an
(Commentary of the Qur'an, in two volumes)

Allahu Akbar
(God is Great, in Urdu)

Al-Islam Yatahadda
(Modern Challenges to Islam, in Arabic)

A TREASURY OF
THE QUR'AN

BOOK ONE: THE GOOD LIFE

COMPILED BY
MAULANA WAHIDUDDIN KHAN

Goodword
B · O · O · K · S

GOODWORD BOOKS
1, Nizamuddin West Market
New Delhi 110 013
Tel. 435 5454, 435 6666, 435 1128.
Fax 435 7333, 435 7980
E-mail: info@goodwordbooks.com
www.goodwordbooks.com

CONTENTS

INTRODUCTION

This book comprises excerpts from the Qur'ān, arranged under relevant headings. It provides an introduction to Islam which is derived directly from the original, revealed source. No interpretation or commentary has been added.

The theme of this book—the good life—is taken from the following verse of the Qur'ān:

> Be they men or women those who believe and do what is right, We shall surely endow with a good life: We shall reward them according to their noblest actions (16:97).

The meaning of the "good life" mentioned in this verse is clear from the phrase "according to their noblest actions." A good life is a life of good actions. A commentator of the Qur'ān, aḍ-Ḍaḥḥāk, has defined it as "being content with an honest living and serving God in one's life." This is the meaning that the Companions of the Prophet and their followers generally inferred from the phrase.

To believe in God and implement His commandments is to qualify oneself for His succour. God bestows multiple blessings on a person who lives a life of faith and righteousness. He enables him to experience the joy of closeness to God in his worship; to settle day-to-day problems in a divinely-inspired manner; to deal with friends and foes in an equally honest-to-God way, God guides him on the straight path. He in turn always seeks God's pleasure and nothing can turn him away from this aim.

The Qur'ān has given a clear exposition of the theoretical and practical nature of the good life. The verses which have been selected for this book describe various fundamental aspects of this life in the Qur'ān's inimitable style. These passages thus provide both a description of the good life and an authentic example of how it should be lived.

Wahiduddin Khan
The Islamic Centre, New Delhi

GOD IS ONE

Say: God is One, The Eternal God. He begot none, nor was He begotten. None is equal to Him.

(112:1-4)

Mankind, worship your Lord, who has created you and those before you so that you may ward off evil; who has made the earth a couch for you and the sky a canopy; and has sent down water from the sky, thereby producing fruits for you to eat. So do not knowingly set up rivals to God.

(2:21-22)

God forgives not that partners should be ascribed unto Him. He forgives whom He will all other sins. Whoever ascribes partners unto God has strayed far from the truth.

(4:116)

GOD—THE SUBLIME,
THE TREMENDOUS

Allah—there is no deity save Him, the Ever-living, the Eternal. Neither slumber nor sleep overtakes Him. To Him belongs all that is in the heavens and the earth. Who can intercede with Him save by His leave? He knows what lies before humans and what is after them, and they encompass nothing of His knowledge save what He wills. His throne comprises both the heavens and the earth, and He is never weary of preserving them. He is the Sublime the Tremendous.

(2:255)

GOD'S SIGNS

Your Lord is God, who created the skies and the earth in six periods, then ascended His Throne. He throws the veil of night over day. Swiftly they follow one another. The sun, moon and stars are subservient by His command. His is the creation, His is the command. Blessed be God, the Lord of the worlds. Call on your Lord humbly and secretly; He does not love the transgressors. Do not work corruption in the land after things have been set right. Pray to Him fearfully, eagerly. God's mercy is within reach of the righteous. He sends forth the winds as harbingers of His mercy till, when they bear a heavy cloud, We drive it to a dead land and cause rain to descend thereon, bringing forth all manner of fruit. Thus We will raise the dead to life; perchance you will take heed. And as for the good land, its vegetation comes forth by the leave of its Lord. But poor and scant are the fruits which spring from barren soil. Thus We make plain Our signs for those who render thanks. (7:54-58)

In Space and on Earth

So glory be to God morning and evening.
Praise be to Him in space and on earth, at
twilight and at noon. He brings forth the living
from the dead, and the dead from the living, and
He revives the earth after it is dead. Likewise
you shall be raised to life. And of His signs is
that He created you from dust; now behold you
are human beings, ranging widely. And of His
signs is that He created for you, of yourselves,
spouses that you might find repose in them and
has planted love and kindness in your hearts.
Surely there are signs in this for people who
reflect. And of His signs are the creation of the
heavens and the earth and the variety of your
tongues and hues. Surely there are signs in this
for those who know. And of His signs is your
slumbering by night and day, and your seeking
of His bounty. Surely in that are signs for those
who hear. The lightning which He shows you

for fear and hope is yet another of His signs, He sends down water from the sky, thereby reviving the earth after it is dead. Surely in this there are signs for a people who understand. Space and the earth are firm by His command; then when He calls you, suddenly, from the earth you shall emerge. To Him belongs everything in the heavens and on earth; all are obedient to Him. He it is who originates creation, then reproduces it, and it is easier for Him. His is the loftiest likeliness in space and on earth. He is the Mighty, the Wise.

(30:17-27)

THE COSMIC CALL

It is God who splits the grain and the date
stone. He brings forth the living from the dead,
and the dead from the living. Such is God. How
then can you turn away from Him? He splits the
sky into dawn. He has made the night for a
repose and the sun and the moon for a
reckoning. Such is the ordinance of God, the
Mighty, the Wise. It is He who has created for
you the stars, that you may be guided by them
in the darkness of land and sea. We have made
plain our signs for people who understand. It is
He who sent down water from the sky. With it
We bring forth the shoot of every plant and then
We have brought forth its green leaf and from it
close-compounded grain; and out of the date-
palm, from its pollen, dates thick-clustered,
ready to the hand; and gardens of grapes, olives
and pomegranates, like and unlike one another.
Look upon their fruits when they fructify and

ripen. Surely in all this are signs for people who believe. Yet they ascribe as partners unto Him the jinn, though He created them, and they impute unto Him sons and daughters without any knowledge. Glory be to Him and exalted be He above what they describe. The Creator of the heavens and the earth. How can He have a son, when there is for Him no consort; when He created all things and He has knowledge of all things?

(6:96-104)

LORD OF THE GREAT THRONE

Did you think that We created you in vain and that you would never be returned to Us? Exalted be God, the true Master. There is no deity save Him, the Lord of the great throne. And whoever invokes any other deity besides God—a deity of whose divinity he has no proof—with his Lord alone will be his reckoning. The unbelievers shall never prosper. And say: Lord, forgive and have mercy, for You are the best of those that show mercy.

(23:115-118)

LOVE FOR GOD

In the creation of the heavens and the earth; in the alternation of night and day; in the ships that sail the ocean with cargoes beneficial to men; in the water which God sends down from the sky and with which He revives the dead earth after its death, dispersing in it all kinds of beasts; in the swirling of the winds and in the clouds that are driven between earth and sky; surely in this there are signs for people who understand. Yet there are some people who choose from other beings besides God, as rivals to God, loving them as God alone should be loved—whereas those who believe love God more than all else. If the evil-doers could only see, when they behold the doom, that power lies with God alone and that God is severe in punishment. When those who were followed disown their followers and they behold the doom, and their cords are cut asunder. Those who followed will say, "If only a return were possible for us, we would disown them, as they have disowned us." Thus God will show them their own work as anguish for them. They shall never emerge from the Fire. Mankind, eat of what is in the earth lawful and wholesome, and follow not in the steps of Satan, for he is your sworn enemy. He commands you only to evil and indecency and that you should assert about God what you do not know.

(2:164-169)

GOD'S PROPHETS

Those who believe and have not obscured their
belief with wrong-doing are truly secure and
they are rightly guided. Such was the argument
with which We furnished Abraham against his
people. We raise whom We will to an exalted
rank. Your Lord is Wise, All-Knowing. And
We gave to him Isaac and Jacob; each one We
guided as We had guided Noah before them.
And of his progeny David and Solomon, Job
and Joseph, Moses and Aaron; thus We reward
those who do good. And Zachariah and John,
Jesus and Elias; each was of the Righteous. And
Ishmael and Elisha, Jonah and Lot, each one
We preferred above all beings. And of their
fathers and of their offsprings and of their
brethren; We elected them and guided them to a
straight Path. Such is God's guidance. He
bestows it on whom He pleases of His servants.
But if they had served other gods besides Him

their labours would have been in vain. On them We bestowed the scriptures, wisdom and prophethood. If these disbelieve therein, then We shall entrust them to others who are not disbelievers. These are the ones whom God guided. Follow their guidance, and say; I ask no wage for it; it is but a reminder to all beings.

(6:82-90)

HEAVEN AND HELL

They underrate the might of God. But on the
Day of Resurrection He will hold the entire
earth in His grasp and fold up the skies in His
right hand. Glory be to Him! Exalted be He
above all that they associate. The Trumpet shall
be blown and whoever is in the heavens and
whoever is in the earth shall swoon, save whom
God wills. Then it shall be blown a second time
and they will stand and look around them. The
earth will shine with the light of its Lord and
the Book will be set in place. The prophets and
witnesses shall be brought in and all shall be
judged with fairness: none shall be wronged.
Each soul shall be paid in full for what it has
wrought, for He is well-aware of what they do.
Then the disbelievers will be driven into Hell in
companies. When they draw near, its gates will
be opened, and its keepers will say to them:
"Did not messengers come to you from among
yourselves, reciting to you the signs of your

Lord and warning you of the meeting of this day?" They shall say: "Yes, indeed." And thus the punishment which the unbelievers have been promised shall be fulfilled. It shall be said: "Enter the gates of Hell, to dwell therein forever." Evil is the dwelling-place of the arrogant. Then those who feared their Lord shall be led into heaven in companies to Paradise. When they draw near, its gates will be opened and its keepers shall say: "Peace be upon you! Well you have done. Enter Paradise and dwell therein forever." They will say: "Praise be to God, Who has been true to His promise to us and has made us inherit the land, that we may dwell wherever we wish in Paradise." How excellent is the wage of those that labour. And you will see the angels encircling about the Throne, hymning the praises of their Lord. Mankind will be judged with fairness and it will be said: "Praise be to God, Lord of the Worlds."

(39:67-75)

PRAYERS

Perform the prayers at sunset, at nightfall and at dawn; the dawn prayer is witnessed. And pray for a part of the night, an additional duty for you; it may be that your Lord will raise you up to an honourable station.

(17:78-79)

Be constant in praying at the beginning and the end of the day, and in the night too. Good deeds make amends for sins. That is a reminder for the mindful. Therefore have patience; God will not leave to waste the reward of the righteous.

(11:114-115)

And when you have performed the prayer, remember God, standing, sitting and lying down. Then, when you are secure, perform the prayer, for prayer is a duty incumbent on the faithful, to be observed at appointed hours.

(4:103)

Recite what has been revealed to you of the Book, and perform the prayer; prayer prevents indecency and the evil. God's remembrance is greatest of all. And God knows what you do.

(29:45)

Be ever mindful of prayers, and of the midmost prayer. And stand obedient to God.

(2:238)

FASTING

Believers, fasting is prescribed for you, as it was prescribed for those before you, so that you may ward off evil. Fast a certain number of days; but if any of you be sick or on a journey, then a similar number of other days, and it is incumbent upon those who can afford it to make sacrifice by feeding a needy person. Yet it is better for him who does good of his own accord; and that you should fast is better for you, if you but knew it. In the month of Ramadan the Qur'ān was revealed, a guidance for mankind with clear proofs of guidance distinguishing right from wrong. So those of you who witness the month should fast it. But anyone who is sick or on a journey may fast a similar number of other days. God desires ease for you, not hardship. He desires you to fulfill the number and magnify God for having guided you and He wishes you to render thanks.

(2:183-186)

ALMS-GIVING

Believers, spend of that with which We have provided you, before there comes a day when there shall be neither trading, nor friendship nor intercession. Truly it is the unbelievers who are the wrongdoers.

(2:254)

He who spends his wealth in the way of God is like a grain of corn that sprouts seven ears, in every ear a hundred grains. God gives abundance to whom He wills; God is munificent and all-knowing. Those who spend their wealth in the way of God then do not follow up what they spend with reproach and injury shall be rewarded by their Lord; they shall have nothing to fear or regret. A kind word with forgiveness is better than almsgiving followed by injury. God is self-sufficient and clement. Believers, do not mar your almsgiving with reproach and injury, like those who spend their wealth only to be seen and praised by people, and believe neither in God nor in the Last Day. Such people are like a rock covered with a little earth; a shower falls upon it and leaves it hard and bare. They shall gain nothing from their works. God does not guide the unbelievers. But those who give away their wealth from a desire to please God and strengthen their souls are like a garden on a hillside; if a rainstorm falls upon it, it yields up twice its normal crop; and if no rain falls upon it, it is watered by the dew. God sees what you do. Would any of you, being a man well-advanced in age with helpless children to support, wish to have his garden—a garden planted with palm-trees, vines and all manner of fruits, and watered by running streams—blasted and consumed by a fiery whirlwind? Thus God makes plain to you His revelation, so that you may give thought. Believers, give in alms of the wealth you have lawfully earned and of that which We Have brought out of the earth for you; not of worthless things which you yourselves would only reluctantly accept. Know that God is self-sufficient and glorious. Satan threatens you with poverty and bids you unto indecency. But God promises you His forgiveness and bounty. God is munificent and all-knowing. He gives wisdom to whom He wills; and whoever is granted wisdom receives great good. But none take heed except people of understanding.

(2:261-269)

PILGRIMAGE

Perform the pilgrimage and visit the Sacred
House for God's sake. If you are prevented,
send such offerings as you can afford, and do
not shave your heads until the offerings have
reached their destination. But if any of you is ill
or suffers from an ailment of the head, he must
pay a ransom either by fasting or by almsgiving
or by offering a sacrifice. In peacetime if any of
you combines the visit with the pilgrimage he
must make such offerings as he can afford; but
if he lacks the means let him fast three days
during the pilgrimage and seven when he has
returned; that is, ten days in all. That is for him
whose family are not present at the Holy
Mosque. Have fear of God: Know that He is
stern in retribution. Pilgrimage is in the
appointed months. Whoever intends to perform
it in those months must abstain from sexual
intercourse, obscence language and acrimonious

disputes while on pilgrimage. God is aware of whatever good you do. Provide yourselves well; the best provision is piety. Fear Me, then, you that are endowed with understanding. It is no offence for you to seek the bounty of your Lord by trading. When you press on from 'Arafat remember God as you approach the Sacred Monument. Remember Him who gave you guidance when you were in error. Then press on from where people press on, and implore the forgiveness of God. He is forgiving and merciful. And when you have fulfilled your holy rites remember God as you remember your fathers or yet more devoutly. There are some who say: "Lord, give us abundance in this world." These shall have no share in the world to come. But there are others who say: "Lord, give us what is good both in this world and in the next and save us from the doom of Hell." These shall have a share of the reward. Swift is the reckoning of God. Remember God during the appointed days. He that departs on the second day incurs no sin, nor does he who stays longer, if he truly fears God. Have fear of God, then, and know that you shall be gathered before Him.

(2:196:203)

SACRIFICE

For every nation We have appointed a holy rite
that they may pronounce the name of God over
the beasts which He has given them for food.
Your God is One God; so surrender to Him.
And give good news to the humble, whose
hearts tremble with awe at the mention of God;
who endure their misfortunes with fortitude,
attend to their prayers and spend of that which
We have bestowed on them. And as for the
sacrifice of cattle, We have ordained it for you
as one of the symbols set up by God. They are
of much use to you. So pronounce God's name
over them as you draw them up in line and
slaughter them; and when they have fallen
down, eat of their flesh, and feed with it the
poor person and the beggar. So We have
subjected them to you that you may be thankful.
Their flesh and blood does not reach God; it is
your piety that reaches Him. So He has

subjected them to you, that you may magnify God for having guided you. And give good news to the righteous.

(22:34-37)

SERVING GOD

To God belongs all that the heavens and the earth contain. Whether you reveal your thoughts or hide them, God will bring you to account for them. He will forgive whom He will and punish whom He will; He has power over all things. The Prophet believes in what has been revealed to him by his Lord and so do the faithful. They all believe in God and His angels, His scriptures and His prophets. "We make no distinction between any of His prophets," they say: "We hear and We obey. Forgive us, Lord; unto You shall we return." God does not charge a soul with more than it can bear. It shall be requited for whatever good and whatever evil it has done, "Lord do not take us to task if we forget or lapse into error. Lord, do not lay on us the burden You laid on those before us. Lord, do not charge us with more than we can bear. Pardon us, forgive us, and have mercy on us, You alone are our Protector. Help us against the unbelievers." (2:284-286)

THE SHARI'AH

The Lord has enjoined you to worship none but
Him, and to show kindness unto parents. If
either or both of them reach old age with you,
show them no sign of impatience, nor rebuke
them; but speak kindly unto them. Treat them
with humility and tenderness and say: "Lord, be
merciful to them even as they cherished and
reared me when I was an infant." Your Lord
knows best what is in your hearts. If you are
righteous, He is Forgiving to those who turn to
Him again and again. Give to the near of kin
their due, and also to the destitute and to the
wayfarers. Do not squander your substance
wastefully, for the wasteful are Satan's brothers;
and Satan is ever ungrateful to his Lord. But if,
while waiting for your Lord's bounty, then at
least speak to them kindly. Be neither miserly or
prodigal, for then you should either be
reproached or reduced to penury. Your Lord

gives abundantly to whom He wills and sparingly to whom He pleases. He knows and observes His servants. Slay not your children for fear of want. We will provide for them and for you. To kill them is a great sin. Do not approach adultery, for it is an indecent and evil way. Do not slay any person whom God has forbidden you to kill except for a just cause. If someone is slain unjustly, to his heir We have given the right of retaliation. But let him not carry his vengeance too far, for his victim in turn will be assisted and avenged. Do not interfere with the property of orphans except with the best of motives, until they reach maturity. Keep your promises; you are accountable for all that you promise. Give full measure when you measure and weigh with even scales; that is fair and better in the end. Do not pursue what you do not know; man's eyes, ears and heart—each of his senses will be

closely questioned. Do not walk in the earth
with haughty self-conceit; you cannot cleave the
earth, nor can you rival the mountains in stature.
All this is evil; odious in the sight of your Lord.
These injunctions are but a part of the wisdom
with which your Lord has inspired you. Do not
appoint another god with God, or you will be
cast into Hell, reproached and rejected.

(17:23-39)

41

THE SERVANTS OF THE MERCIFUL

The true servants of the Merciful are those who walk upon the earth modestly and say: "Peace!" to the ignorant who address them; who pass the night standing and prostrate in adoration of their Lord; who say: "Lord ward off from us the punishment of Hell, for its punishment is everlasting, an evil dwelling and an evil resting-place"; who, when they spend, are neither wasteful nor niggardly, but keep the golden mean; who invoke no other god besides God, and do not kill save for a just cause; who do not commit adultery. He that does this shall meet with evil: his punishment shall be doubled on the Day of Resurrection and in disgrace he shall abide forever—unless he repent and believe and do good works, for then God will change his sins to good actions; God is Forgiving and Merciful: he that repents and does good works truly returns to God; who do not bear false

witness and when they pass by idle talk, pass by
with dignity; who do not turn a blind eye and a
deaf ear to the revelations of their Lord when
they are reminded of them; who say: "Lord,
give us joy in our spouses and offspring, and
make us examples to those who are God-
fearing." These shall be rewarded with the
highest heaven for their patient endurance.
There they shall be welcomed with a greeting
and peace, and there they shall abide forever; a
blessed dwelling and a blessed resting place.

(25:63-76)

TRUST IN GOD

There is but one God. In Him let the believers
put their trust. Believers, you have an enemy in
your spouses and children: beware of them. But
if you overlook their offences and forgive and
pardon them, then know that God is Forgiving
and Merciful. Your wealth and children are but
a temptation. God's reward is great. Therefore
fear Him as far as you are able and be attentive,
obedient and charitable for the good of your
own selves; for those who are guarded from
their own avarice will surely prosper. If you
give God a generous loan. He will repay you
twofold and will forgive you, for God is Ever
Responsive to gratitude and Most Forbearing.

(64:13-18)

WORDS OF WISDOM

Luqmān admonished his son: "My son," he said, "do not associate other with God; to associate other with God is a mighty sin." We have charged man concerning his parents, for with much pain his mother bears him and he is not weaned before he is two years of age. Give thanks to Me and to your parents. To Me all things shall return. But if they press you to associate with Me, what you know nothing of, then obey them not. Be kind to them in this world, but follow the way of him who turns to me. To me you shall return and I shall tell you what you have done. "My dear son, God will bring all things to light, be they as small as a grain of mustard seed, be they hidden inside a rock or in space or on earth. God is Wise and All-Knowing. My dear son, be steadfast in prayer, enjoin good and forbid evil. Endure with fortitude whatever befalls you. That is true constancy. Do not treat people with scorn, nor walk haughtily on earth; God does not love the arrogant and the vainglorious. Rather let your gait be modest and your voice be low; the ugliest of all voices is the voice of the ass."

(31:13-19)

GOD-FEARING PEOPLE

They ask you about the spoils. Say: "The spoils belong to God and the Messenger. So fear God and settle your disputes. Obey God and His Messenger if you are true believers." The true believers are those whose hearts tremble with awe at the mention of God, and whose faith grows stronger as they listen to His revelations. They put their trust in their Lord, pray steadfastly, and give in alms of that which We have given them. Such are the true believers. They shall be exalted and forgiven by their Lord, and a generous provision shall be made for them.

(8:1-4)

THE GOOD LIFE

God enjoins justice, kindness and charity to
one's kindred, and forbids indecency,
abomination and oppression. He admonishes
you so that you may take heed. Keep faith with
God when you make a covenant with Him. Do
not break your oaths after having confirmed
them and having called upon God to be your
surety. God has knowledge of your actions. Do
not, like the woman who unravels to bits the
thread which she has firmly spun, take oaths
with mutual deceit and break them on finding
yourselves superior to others in numbers. In this
God puts you to the proof. On the Day of
Resurrection He will make clear to you that
over which you are at variance. Had God
willed, He would have united you into one
community. But He leaves in error whom He
wills and guides whom He wills. You shall be
questioned about your actions. Do not take oaths

to deceive each other, lest your foot should slip after it has stood firm, and lest evil should befall you for debarring others from the path of God, and lest there should await you a mighty punishment.

Do not sell covenant of God for a trifling price. That which is with God is better for you, if you but knew it. Your worldly riches are transitory, but that which is with God is everlasting. We shall reward the steadfast according to their noblest deeds. Be they men or women, those who believe and do what is right We shall surely endow with a good life; We shall reward them according to their noblest actions.

(16:90-97)

HARĀM AND HALĀL

Say: "Come, I will tell you what your Lord has made binding on you: that you ascribe no partner unto Him: that you show kindness to your parents; that you slay not your children because of poverty; We provide for you and for them; that you commit not any shameful deeds, openly or secretly; that you slay not the soul God has prohibited except by right. Thus God exhorts you, that you may grow in wisdom. Do not touch the property of orphans, but strive to improve their lot until they reach maturity. Give just weight and full measure; We never charge a soul with more than it can bear. When you speak, be just, even though it be against a relative. Be true to God's covenant. Thus God exhorts you, so that you may take heed.

(6:151-152)

Say: "My Lord has forbidden only shameful deeds, whether outward or inward, and sin and wrongful oppression; and that you associate with God that for which no warrant has been revealed, or to tell of God what you do not know. Every nation has its term; when their hour comes they shall not put it back by a single hour nor put it forward. Children of Adam, when apostles of your own come to proclaim to you My revelations, those that take warning and mend their ways will have nothing to fear or to regret; but those that deny and scorn Our revelations shall be inhabitants of the Fire, and there they shall remain forever.

(7:33-36)

HEAVENLY SOULS

Indeed man was born with a restless disposition.
When evil befalls him he is filled with self-pity,
but blessed with good fortune he grows
niggardly. Not so the worshippers who are
steadfast in their prayer; who set aside a due
portion of their goods for the needy and the
dispossessed; who truly believe in the Day of
Reckoning and dread the punishment of their
Lord for none is secure from the punishment of
God; who preserve their chastity save with their
wives and slave girls, for in their case they are
not blameworthy; but those who lust after other
than those are transgressors; who keep their
trusts and promises and bear true witness; and
who attend to their prayers. These shall be in
Gardens, honoured.

(70:19-35)

THE SERENE SOUL

As for man, when his Lord tests him by honouring him and bestowing favours on him, he says: "My Lord has honoured me." But when He tests him by straitening his means of life, he says: "My Lord despises me." No! but you show no kindness to the orphan, and do not urge one another to feed the poor. Greedily you devour inheritance, and you love riches with all your hearts. No! But when the earth is crushed to fine dust, and your Lord comes, and the angels rank on rank, and Hell is brought near, on that Day man will take heed but what good will it do him now? He will say: "Would that I had sent before me some provision for my life." But on that Day none will punish as He will punish, nor will any bind with chains like His. Serene soul, return to your Lord, well-pleased and pleasing Him. Join My servants and enter My Paradise.

(89:15-30)

DIVINE SOULS

Believers, do not devour usury, doubling. Have fear of God and you shall prosper. Guard youselves against the fire of Hell prepared for unbelievers. Obey God and the Prophet that you may find mercy. Vie with each other to earn the forgiveness of your Lord and a Paradise as vast as heaven and earth, prepared for the righteous; those who give alms alike in prosperity and adversity; who curb their anger and forgive their fellow people. God loves the charitable. And who, if they commit evil or wrong their souls, remember God and seek forgiveness for their sins—who but God forgives sins—and do not knowingly persist in their misdeeds. These shall be rewarded with forgiveness from their Lord and Gardens underneath which running streams flow, where they shall dwell forever, How excellent is the wage of those who labour.

(3:130-136)

THE CORRECT WAY

That which you have been given is but the fleeting comfort of this life. For better and more enduring is God's reward to those who believe and put their trust in Him; who avoid gross sins and indecencies and, when angered, are willing to forgive; who respond to the call of their Lord, are constant in prayer, and conduct their affairs by mutual consent; who bestow in alms a portion of that which We have given them and, when oppressed, seek to redress their wrongs. Let evil be rewarded with like evil. But he who forgives and seeks reconcilement shall be rewarded by God. He does not love the wrongdoers. Those who avenge themselves when wronged incur no guilt. But great is the guilt of those who oppress their fellow people and conduct themselves with wickedness and injustice. These shall be sternly punished. But true constancy lies in forgiveness and patient forebearance.   (42:36-43)

PROFITABLE TRADING

Believers, shall I point out to you a profitable
trade that will save you from a painful doom?
Believe in God and His Messenger and strive
for His cause with your wealth and your lives.
That would be best for you, if you only knew it.
He will forgive you your sins and admit you to
Gardens, underneath which running streams
flow; He will lodge you in pleasant mansions in
the Gardens of Eden. That is the supreme
triumph. And (He will bestow upon you) other
blessings which you desire: help from God and
a speedy victory. Give the good news to the
faithful. Believers, be God's helpers. When
Jesus, the son of Mary, said to his disciples:
"Who will help me on the way to God?" They
replied: "We are God's helpers." Then some of
the Israelites believed in him while others did
not. We helped the believers against their
enemies and they triumphed over them.

(61:10-14)

REAL PIETY

Piety does not consist in turning your faces towards the east or the west. The pious are those who believe in God and in the Last Day, in the angels and the scriptures and the prophets; who for the love of God give their wealth to kins-folk, orphans, the poor, wayfarers and beggars, and for the redemption of captives; who attend to the prayers and pay the poor-due; who are true to their promises and endure with fortitude misfortune, hardships and peril. These are the true believers, these are the God-fearing.

(2:177)

GOD'S HOSPITALITY

Do the unbelievers think that they can make
My servants as protectors against Me? We have
prepared Hell to be their dwelling place. Say:
"Shall we tell you who will lose most through
their labours? Those whose endeavours in this
world are misguided and who yet think that
what they do is right; who disbelieve the
revelations of their Lord and deny that they will
ever meet Him." Vain are their works. On the
Day of Resurrection We shall assign no weight
to them. Hell is their reward: because they had
no faith and scoffed at My messengers and My
signs. As for those who have faith and do good
works, the Gardens of Paradise shall be their
hospitality. They shall dwell there forever,
desiring no change to befall them. Say: "If all
the sea were ink with which to write the words
of my Lord, the sea would surely be consumed
before my Lord's words were finished, though

we brought another sea to replenish it." Say: "I am but a mortal like yourselves. It is revealed to me that your Lord is One God. Let those that hope to meet their Lord do what is right and make none sharer of the worship due to his Lord.

(18:102-110)

THE BELIEVER'S LIVELIHOOD

Believers, when you are summoned to Friday
prayers hasten to the remembrance of God and
cease your trading. That would be best for you,
if you but knew it. Then, when the prayer is
ended, scatter in the land and go in quest of
God's bounty. Remember God always, so that
you may prosper. But when they see some
merchandise or passing delight they flock to it
eagerly, leaving you alone. Say: "That which
God has in store is far better than passing
delight and merchandise. God is the best
of providers."

(62:9-11)

THE PEOPLE OF PARADISE

Truly successful are the believers who are
humble in their prayers; who avoid profanity,
and are active in charitable works; who restrain
their carnal desires, except with their wives and
slavegirls for these are lawful to them but
whoever seeks after more than that has
transgressed; who are true to their trusts and
promises and never neglect their prayers. These
are the inheritors; who shall inherit the Paradise,
and therein they shall abide forever.

(23:1-11)

EVERYTHING FOR GOD

God has bought from the believers their selves
and their possessions and in return has promised
them Paradise. They fight for His cause, slay,
and are slain. That is a promise binding upon
God in the Torah, the Gospel and the Qur'ān.
And who is more true to his promise than God:
Rejoice, then, in the bargain you have made.
That is the supreme triumph. Those who repent,
those who worship, those who praise Him, those
who journey, those who bow down, those who
prostrate themselves, those who enjoin right,
forbid wrong, and observe the commandments
of God, shall be richly rewarded. Give the good
news to the believers.

(9:111-112)

THE BELIEVER IS GOD'S TREE

Do you not see how God compares a good word to a good tree? Its root is firm and its branches are in the sky; it yields its fruit in every season by God's leave. God gives people parables so that they may take heed. But an evil word is like an evil tree torn out of the earth, possessing no stability. God will strengthen the faithful with (His) steadfast Word, both in this life and the hereafter. He leads the wrongdoers astray. He accomplishes what He pleases.

(14:24-27)

GOOD ADVICE

God commands you to hand back your trusts to
their rightful owners, and to pass judgement
upon people with fairness. Noble is the advice
God gives you. He hears all and observes all.

(4:58)

He who fears God will take heed, but the most
hapless will flout the warning. He shall be cast
into the great Fire, where he shall neither die
nor live. Successful is he who purifies himself,
who remembers the name of his Lord and prays.
Yet you prefer the life of this world, although
the life to come is better and more lasting.

(87:10-17)

DOOMED TO DESTRUCTION

Woe to every backbiting slanderer who amass riches and sedulously hoard them, thinking that his riches will render him immortal! By no means! He shall be flung to the Destroying torment. Would that you knew what the Destroying torment was like! It is God's own kindled fire, which will rise up to people's hearts. It will close upon them from every side, in endless columns.

(104:1-9)

THE DENIERS OF GOD'S SIGNS

He who turns away from My rememberance
shall live in anguish and come before Us blind
on the Day of Resurrection. "Lord," he will say,
"why have you brought me blind before you
when in my lifetime I was blessed with sight?"
God will answer: "Because Our signs came unto
you and you forgot them. In like manner this
Day you are yourself forgotten." And thus do
We reward the transgressor who denies the
revelations of his Lord. But the punishment of
the world to come is more terrible and
more lasting.

(20:124-127)

FAIR TESTIMONY

Believers, be ever steadfast in your devotion to God, bearing fair testimony. Do not allow hatred for some people to turn you away from justice. Deal justly; justice is nearer to piety. Have fear of God; He knows what you do. God has promised those who believe and do good works forgiveness and a rich reward. And the unbelievers who deny Our signs shall dwell in Hell.

(5:8-10)

LIVING IN HARMONY

Believers, when you confront an opposing force
stand firm and make constant mention of God,
so that you may triumph. Obey God and His
Messenger and do not quarrel with one another,
lest you should lose courage and your resolve
weaken. Have patience; God is with those who
are patient. Do not be like those who left their
homelands elated with arrogance and a desire to
be seen and praised by men. They debar others
from the path of God: but God encompasses
what they do.

(8:45-47)

ISLAMIC SOCIETY

Believers, if an ungodly person brings you
some news inquire first into its truth, lest you
should hurt others unwittingly and, afterwards
be filled with remorse for what you have done.
Know that God's Messenger is among you. If
he obeyed you in many matters, you would
surely come to grief. But God has endeared the
Faith to you and beautified it in your hearts,
making unbelief, wrongdoing and disobedience
abhorrent to you. Such are those who are rightly
guided through God's grace and blessing. God
is wise and all-knowing. If two parties of the
believers take up arms against one another,
make peace between them. If either of them
commits aggression against the other, fight
against the aggressors until they submit to
God's judgement. When they submit, make
peace between them in equity and justice; God
loves the just. The believers are one

brotherhood; make peace among your brothers and fear God, so that you may be shown mercy. Believers, let no men mock other men who may perhaps be better than the former. Let no women mock other women, who may perhaps be better than the former. Do not defame one another, nor call one another by nicknames. It is evil to be called by a bad name after embracing the true faith. Those who do not repent are wrongdoers. Believers, avoid much suspicion for in some cases suspicion is a sin. Do not spy on one another, nor backbite one another. Would any of you like to eat the flesh of his dead brother? Surely you would loathe it. Have fear of God. He is forgiving and merciful. Mankind, We have created you from a male and a female and divided you into nations and tribes, that you may know one another. The noblest of you in God's sight is the one who fears God most. God is wise, all-knowing.

(49:6-13)

CALLING TO GOD

Call to the way of your Lord with wisdom and goodly exhortation. Argue with them in the most kindly manner. Your Lord knows best those who stray from His path and those who are rightly guided. If you punish, let your punishment be proportionate to the wrong that has been done to you. But it is best for you to endure your wrong with patience. So be patient; your patience is for God. Do not grieve over them, and neither be distressed by their plots. God is with those who keep from evil and do good works.

(16:125-128)

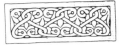

MAGNIFYING THE LORD

You who are wrapped up in your vestment, arise and warn, Magnify your Lord, purify your innerself. Keep away from all pollution. Be patient, for your Lord's sake. The day when the trumpet sounds should not be an easy one for the unbelievers; it shall be a day of anguish for them.

(74:1-10)

Nay, by the moon! By the departing night and the rising dawn, Hell is a dire scourge, a warning to mankind; alike to those of you who would advance and those that would hang back. Each soul is the hostage of its own deeds. But those on the right hand—they will be in their gardens, inquiring of the sinners; "What brought you into the Fire?" They will reply: "We never prayed or fed the hungry. We engaged in vain disputes and denied the Day of Reckoning until death overtook us." No intercessor's plea shall avail them then.

(74:32-48)

ETERNITY IS BETTER

Successful is the person who purifies himself,
who remembers the name of his Lord, and
prays. Yet you prefer this life, although the life
to come is better and more lasting. All this is
written in earlier scriptures; the scriptures of
Abraham and Moses.

(87:14-19)

THEIR EFFORTS WILL BE REWARDED

We have created man from a drop of thickened
fluid so that We may test him. We made him a
being endowed with hearing and sight. We have
shown him the way, whether he be grateful or
ungrateful. For the unbelievers We have
prepared fetters and chains, and a blazing fire.
But the righteous shall drink a cup flavoured
with the Camphor—a gushing spring at which
the servants of God will refresh themselves
making it gush forth abundantly; they who keep
their vows and dread the far-spread terrors of
Judgement Day; who, though they hold it dear,
give sustenance to the poor person, the orphan
and the captive, saying: 'We feed you for God's
sake alone; we seek of you neither recompense
nor thanks; for we fear from Him a day of
anguish and of woe." God will deliver them
from the evil of that day, and will make their
faces shine with joy. He will reward them for

their steadfastness with robes of silk and the delights of Paradise. Reclining there upon soft couches, they shall feel neither the scorching heat not the biting cold. Trees will spread their shade around them, and fruit will hang in clusters over them. They shall be served with silver dishes, and beakers as large as goblets; silver goblets which they themselves shall measure; and cups brimfull with ginger-flavoured water from the Fount of Salsabīl. They shall be attended by boys graced with eternal youth, who, to the beholder's eyes will seem like sprinkled pearls. When you gaze upon that scene you will behold a kingdom blissful and glorious. They shall be arrayed in garments of fine green silk and rich brocade, and adorned with bracelets of silver. Their Lord will give them pure beverage to drink. Thus you shall be rewarded; since your endeavour in life shall meet with goodly acceptance.

(76:2-22)

THE DAY OF REWARD AND RETRIBUTION

When the sky is cleft asunder; when the stars scatter and the oceans burst beyond their bounds; when the graves are overturned; each soul will know what it has sent ahead and it has left behind. O man! What evil has enticed you away from your gracious Lord who created you, gave you an upright form, and well-proportioned you? In whatever shape He willed, He moulded you. Yes, you deny the Last Judgement. Yet there are guardians watching over you, noble recorders who know of all your actions. The righteous shall surely dwell in Bliss. But the wicked shall burn in a blazing fire on the Judgement-Day; which they shall not be able to evade. Would that you knew what the Day of Judgement is! Oh, would that you knew what the Day of Judgement is! A Day when no soul shall be of the least avail to another soul; for on that Day all sovereignty is God's alone.

(82:1-19)

THE RELIGION THAT IS PLEASING TO GOD

As for the home of the world to come, We shall grant it to those who seek neither to exalt themselves in this world nor yet to spread corruption. The righteous shall have a blessed end. Whoever does good shall be rewarded with what is better. But those who do evil shall be requited only what they did.

(28:83-84)

As for him who rebelled, and preferred the life of this world; Hell shall be his Final Abode. But as for him who feared to stand before his Lord and restrained his soul from base desires; Paradise shall be his Final Abode.

(79:37-41)

He that chooses a religion other than Islam, it will not be accepted from him and in the world to come he will be one of the lost.

(3:85)

PRAYER

Praise be to God, Lord of the Universe, the Compassionate, the Merciful, Master of the Day of Judgement. You alone we worship, and to You alone we ask for help. Guide us to the straight path. The path of those whom You have favoured, not of those who have incurred Your wrath, nor of those who have gone astray.

(I:1-7)

I am God. There is no deity save Me. So serve Me, and perform regular prayers for my remembrance.

(20:14)

To the Lord

Lord, take us not to task if we forget or lapse
into error. Lord, do not lay on us the burden
You laid on those before us. Lord, do not
charge us with more than we can bear. Pardon
us, forgive us our sins, and have mercy upon us.
You alone are our Protector. Give us victory
over the deniers.

(2:286)

God, Lord of all sovereignty, You bestow
sovereignty on whom You will and take it away
from whom You please; You exalt whomever
You will and abase whomever You please. In
Your hand lies all that is good; You have power
over all things. You cause the night to pass into
the day and the day to pass into the night; you
bring forth the living from the dead and the
dead from the living. You give without stint to
whom You will.   (3:26-27)

PROTECT US!

Lord, give us joy in our spouses and offspring,
and cause to be foremost among those who are
God-fearing.

(25:74)

Inspire me, Lord, to render thanks for the
favours you have bestowed on me and on my
parents, and to do good work that will please
You. Admit me, through Your mercy, among
your righteous servants.

(27:19)

Lord, Your mercy and knowledge embrace all
things. Forgive those that repent and follow
Your path. Shield them from the scourge of
Hell. Admit them, Lord, to the Gardens of Eden
which you have promised them, together with
all the righteous among their fathers, their spouses,
and their descendents. You are the Almighty,
the Wise One. Deliver them from all evil. He

whom You will deliver from evil on that Day is
surely one You have graced with Your mercy.
That is the supreme triumph.

(40:7-9)

HELP US!

Lord, give us what is good both in this world
and in the next and save us from the
chastisement of Fire.

(2:201)

Lord, shower us with steadfastness. Make firm
our step and help us against the unbelievers.

(2:250)

Lord, do not cause our hearts to go astray after
You have guided us. Grant us Your own mercy;
You are the munificent Giver.

(3:8)

Lord, we believe in you: forgive us our sins and
keep us from the torment of Hell-fire.

(3:16)

PURIFY OUR HEARTS

Forgive us Lord, and forgive our brothers who
embraced the Faith before us. Do not put in our
hearts any malice towards the faithful. Lord,
You are compassionate, merciful.

(59:10)

Lord, in you we have put our trust; to You we
turn and to You we shall come at last. Lord, do
not expose us to the designs of the unbelievers.
Forgive us, Lord, You are the Mighty, the
Wise One.

(60:4-5)

Lord, perfect our light for us and forgive us.
You have power over all things.

(66:8)

GRANT US A RIGHTEOUS END

Lord, You have not created these in vain. Glory
be to You! Save us from the torment of Hell-
fire. Lord, those whom You will cast into Hell
shall be put to eternal shame: none will help the
wrong-doers. Lord, we have heard a crier
calling men unto Faith, saying: "Believe in your
Lord." So we believed, Lord, then, forgive us
our sins and remove from us our evil deeds and
make us die with the righteous. Lord, grant us
what You promised through your messengers
and do not cast shame on us on the Day of
Resurrection. Verily, You never fail to fulfill
Your promise.

(3:191-194)

HAVE MERCY ON US!

Lord, make me and my descendents steadfast in
prayer. Lord, accept my prayer. Forgive me,
Lord, and forgive my parents and all the faithful
on the Day of Reckoning.

(14:40-41)

Lord, have mercy on them both (i.e., my
parents) as they cherished and cared for me
when I was a little child.

(17:24)

SAVE US FROM EVIL

Lord, we have wronged our souls. Pardon us and have mercy on us, or we shall surely be among the lost.

(7:23)

Lord, shower us with patience and let us die as Muslims (who have surrendered themselves to Your Will).

(7:126)

Lord, You alone are our Guardian. Forgive us and have mercy on us: You are the Best of those who forgive. Ordain for us what is good, both in this life and in the Hereafter. To You we have turned in repentance.

(7:155-156)

Lord, do not let us suffer at the hands of the wicked. Deliver us, through Your mercy, from the unbelievers.

(10:85-86)

Creator of the heavens and earth, You are my
Guardian in this world and in the next. Let me
die as one submitting to Your Will (i.e.,
Muslim) and join the righteous.

(12:101)

STRENGTHEN US!

Lord, grant me a goodly entrance and a goodly exit, and grant me from You a sustaining strength.

(17:80)

Lord, give us mercy from Yourself, and direct us to right conduct in our plight.

(18:10)

LEAVE ME NOT ALONE!

Lord, expand my heart, and ease my task for me. Free my tongue from its impediment, that they may understand my speech.

(20:25-28)

Lord, cause me to grow in knowledge.

(20:114)

Lord, I have been afflicted with distress and You are the Most Merciful of all who show mercy.

(21:83)

Lord, do not leave me alone, You are the Best of all heirs.

(21:89)

Lord, let my landing be blessed. You are the Best of those Who cause people to land.

(23:29)

Lord, build me a house with You in Paradise.

(76:11)

Lord, I stand in need of the blessing which You have sent me.

(28:24)

Lord, deliver me from these corrupt people.

(29:30)

Avenge me, Lord, I am overcome!

(54:10)

SAVE US FROM DOOM

Lord, I seek refuge in You from the promptings of the devils. Lord, I seek refuge in You from their presence.

(23:98-99)

Lord, we believe in You. Forgive us and have mercy on us; You are the Most Merciful.

(23:109)

Lord, ward off from us the punishment of Hell, for its punishment is everlasting.

(25:65)

The Basic Concepts in the Quran
HARUN YAHYA

ONE RELIGION
ZAHEER U. AHMED

Heart of the Koran
Lex Hixon

MY DISCOVERY OF ISLAM
MUHAMMAD ASAD

BASIC THEMES OF THE QURAN
MAULANA ABUL KALAM AZAD

THE HAJJ PILGRIMAGE
BURTON

GCSE ISLAM
The Do-It-Yourself Guide
Ruqaiyyah Waris Maqsood

THE HADITH FOR BEGINNERS
DR. MUHAMMAD ZUBAYR SIDDIQI

The Caliphate
Sir Thomas Arnold

RELIGION OF ISLAM
G.N. AHMED MOULVI

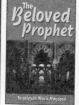
The Beloved Prophet
Ruqaiyyah Waris Maqsood

THE MUSLIM PRAYER ENCYCLOPAEDIA
A COMPLETE GUIDE TO PRAYERS AS TAUGHT BY THE PROPHET MUHAMMAD
Ruqaiyyah Waris Maqsood

How Greek Science Passed to the Arabs
De Lacy O'Leary

ARABIC ENGLISH DICTIONARY FOR ADVANCED LEARNERS
J.E. HAVA

MUHAMMAD A PROPHET FOR ALL HUMANITY
MAULANA WAHIDUDDIN KHAN

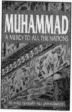
MUHAMMAD A MERCY TO ALL THE NATIONS
AL-HAJ QASSIM ALI JAIRAZBHOY

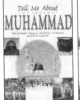

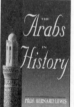

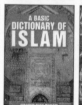

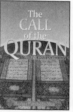

ISLAM AND THE DIVINE COMEDY

MIGUEL ASIN

HARUN YAHYA

EVER THOUGHT ABOUT THE TRUTH?

THE MORAL VALUES OF THE QURAN

HARUN YAHYA

CRUDE UNDERSTANDING OF DISBELIEF

HARUN YAHYA

A Simple Guide to MUSLIM PRAYER

MUHAMMAD MASHUQ AL SIDDIQI

A Simple Guide to ISLAM

FARIDA KHANAM

A Simple Guide to ISLAMIC CONTRIBUTION TO SCIENCE AND CIVILISATION

MAULVI ABDUL KARIM

THE SPREAD OF ISLAM IN FRANCE

MICHEL REEBER

The Essential Arabic

A Learner's Practical Guide

Rafi'el-Imad Faynan

A HISTORY OF ARABIC LITERATURE

CLEMENT HUART

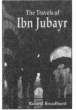
The Travels of Ibn Jubayr

Roland Broadhurst

THE STORY OF ISLAMIC SPAIN

SYED AZIZUR RAHMAN

MUHAMMAD THE HERO AS PROPHET

THOMAS CARLYLE

THE ISLAMIC ART OF PERSIA

A.J. ARBERRY

THE MORISCOS OF SPAIN

HENRY CHARLES LEA

MUHAMMAD A PROPHET FOR ALL HUMANITY

MAULANA WAHIDUDDIN KHAN

Children's Stories from the Quran

The Ark of Nuh
and the Great Flood
Sticker Book

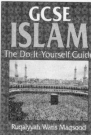

GCSE
ISLAM
The Do-It-Yourself Guide

Ruqaiyyah Waris Maqsood

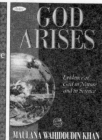

GOD
ARISES

Evidence of God in Nature and in Science

MAULANA WAHIDDUDIN KHAN

ARABIC
ENGLISH
DICTIONARY

J.G. HAVA

THE
Quran
FOR
Astronomy
AND
Earth Exploration from Space

S. Waqar Ahmed Husaini.

ISLAMIC
THOUGHT

IN THE RISE AND SUPREMACY OF ISLAMIC-TECHNOLOGICAL CULTURE:
WATER RESOURCES AND ENERGY

S. WAQAR AHMAD HUSAINI

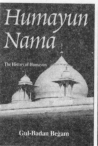

Humayun
Nama

The History of Humayun

Gul-Badan Begam

THE MORISCOS OF
SPAIN

HENRY CHARLES LEA

THE
SPREAD
OF
ISLAM
IN THE WORLD
A History of Peaceful Preaching

Prof. Thomas Arnold